First World War
and Army of Occupation
War Diary
France, Belgium and Germany

40 DIVISION
Divisional Troops
188 Brigade Royal Field Artillery
4 June 1916 - 1 January 1917

WO95/2599/2

The Naval & Military Press Ltd
www.nmarchive.com
Published in association with The National Archives

Published by

The Naval & Military Press Ltd

Unit 10 Ridgewood Industrial Park,

Uckfield, East Sussex,

TN22 5QE England

Tel: +44 (0) 1825 749494

www.naval-military-press.com

www.nmarchive.com

This diary has been reprinted in facsimile from the original. Any imperfections are inevitably reproduced and the quality may fall short of modern type and cartographic standards.

© **Crown Copyright**
Images reproduced by permission of The National Archives, London, England, 2015.

Contents

Document type	Place/Title	Date From	Date To
Heading	WO95/2599/2		
Heading	40th Division 188th Brigade R.F.A. Jun 1916-1917 Jan Broken		
Heading	War Diary Of D Battery 188 Brigade R.F.A. From 4-6-16 To 30-6-16 Volume 1.D/188 RFA June Vol I		
Heading	War Diary Of 188th Brigade R.F.A. From 4.6.16 To 30.6.16 Volume I		
War Diary	Deepcut.	04/06/1916	06/06/1916
War Diary	Nedonchelle	06/06/1916	17/06/1916
War Diary	Le Brebis	18/06/1916	30/06/1916
War Diary	Deepcut		
War Diary	Farnborough	04/06/1916	04/06/1916
War Diary	Harvre	05/06/1916	06/06/1916
War Diary	Berguette	07/06/1916	07/06/1916
War Diary	Nedon	07/06/1916	11/06/1916
War Diary	Noeux-Les-Mines	11/06/1916	11/06/1916
War Diary	N. Maroc	14/06/1916	30/06/1916
Heading	War Diary Of 188th Brigade R.F.A. (left Group 40th D.A) From 1st July 1916 To 31st July 1916 (Volume I.) 40 July 188 R.F.A Vol 2		
War Diary		01/07/1916	31/07/1916
Heading	War Diary Of 188th Brigade R.F.A. From August 1st-August 31st 1916 (Volume I) Vol 3		
War Diary		01/08/1916	31/08/1916
Heading	War Diary Of 188th Bde. R.F.A. From 1st Sept. 1916 To 30th Sept 1916 Volume I Vol 4		
War Diary	0	01/09/1916	30/09/1916
Heading	War Diary Of 188 Brigade R.F.A. From 1st October 1916 To 31st October 1916 Volume I.		
War Diary		01/10/1916	01/01/1917

WO95/2599/2

40TH DIVISION

188TH BRIGADE R.F.A.

JUN 1916 - ~~DEC 1916~~ JUN 1917

Broken up

A/188 RFA
Geese
Vol 1

CONFIDENTIAL

WAR DIARY

of

D BATTERY 188 BRIGADE R.F.A.

from 4-6-16 to 30-6-16

Volume 1.

Jan '16
Dec '16

CONFIDENTIAL.

War Diary
of
188th Brigade R.F.A.

From 4.6.16 to 30.6.16

Volume I.

WAR DIARY
or
INTELLIGENCE SUMMARY

(Erase heading not required.)

Army Form C. 2118

Place	Date	Hour	Summary of Events and Information	Remarks and references to Appendices
Deepcut	4.6.16		The Brigade entrained at Farnborough L.S.W.R Station en route for Southampton as follows :-	
		5.55	½ B. Battery	
		6.30	½ " "	
		8.30	½ C "	
		9.30	½ " "	
		10.30	½ D "	
		11.30	½ " "	
		12.30	½ A "	
		13.45	½ A " + B.H.Q.	
			B Battery on the City of Dunkirk. "A" "C" "D" & "B.H.Q" (each unit divided so as to leave men to attend to horses on S.S. N.W. Miller) embarked on SS N.W. Miller and SS France. Arrive safely at Havre - disembark without casualties by 17 o'clock and move to No 5 Rest camp. Leave Havre.	
	5.6.16	9.59	A Battery and BHQ arrive BERGUET. 4 o'clock 6/6/16.	
	6.6.16	12.-	B. ——— arrives LILLERS	
			C ——— arrives BERGUET	
			D ——— arrives LILLERS.	
	6.6.16		All units proceed to NEDON + NEDONCHELLE MAP 36 B. ⅔. B 7+8.	

WAR DIARY
or
INTELLIGENCE SUMMARY
(Erase heading not required.)

Army Form C. 2118

Instructions regarding War Diaries and Intelligence Summaries are contained in F. S. Regs., Part II. and the Staff Manual respectively. Title Pages will be prepared in manuscript.

Place	Date	Hour	Summary of Events and Information	Remarks and references to Appendices
NEDONCHELLE	6/6/16	13.00	Bde. H.Q. established at point (Sheet France 36B) 1/40000 B.7.C.8.5.	
	10/6/16	7.00	Bde. & Battery commanders leave in Motor Bus with O.O. & one Subaltern from each Battery for NOEUX LES MINES (Sheet 36B) L.25.b.2.2. They report themselves at H.Q. 1st Div Arty. Then proceed to inspect gun positions near LES BREBIS (36B) L.36. On completion of inspection return to NEDONCHELLE.	
"	11/6/16		½ Brigade proceeds to 1st Line. ½ A Bty starts 8 o'clock; ½ B. 8.30; ½ C 9.0; ½ D. 10.0 All Battery commanders go. The following officers are left in charge of ½ Batteries at NEDON. A. Lt Boulton. B. 2/Lt Simpkins C. Lt Rutherford D. Lt Price.	
"	12/6/16		½ Brigade still at NEDONCHELLE receives orders at 23.45 o'clock to proceed to front line.	
"	13/6/16	10.0	Brigade leaves for front line as follows: C Bty leaves starting point Road Junction T.24.c.8.4 (Sheet 36A) at 10 o'clock and proceeds via FAUQUENHEM – LILLERS – BETHUNE – SAILLY LA BOURSE to (36B) L.26.b.1.2 to join 1st Division. Remainder of Bde proceeds as follows: HQ + ½ "A" Battery passes starting point B.4.d.10.7. at 11.20 o'clock & proceeds via CAUCHY A LA TOUR – AUCHEL – MARLES LES MINES – Road junction J.17.6.7.8. NOEUX LES MINES.	

1875 Wt: W593/826 1,000,000 4/15 J.B.C. & A. A.D.S.S./Forms/C. 2118.

WAR DIARY or INTELLIGENCE SUMMARY

Army Form C. 2118

Place	Date	Hour	Summary of Events and Information	Remarks and references to Appendices
	13/6/16		½ B para starting point 11.40 - ½ D para same starting point at 12.0.0 all en route for same destination where guides met the Batteries conducting the horses and drivers to their wagon Lines in NOEUX LES MINES and the gunners to join their Batteries in action at positions Near le Brebis. The Brigade relieved had taken off the wagon covers used as shelter and so Brigade H.Q. did not get any Billets and only reached a place near A Bty wagon line at midnight.	
	14/6/16		The Brigade is in action as follows. Bde H.Q. situated in a villa at Map Reference Sheet 36 B NE 1/20000 L 36 c 0.6 A Bty at L. 36.a.78. (Sheet 36 NE 1/20000) B Batty at G. 26.c. 3. 4 (" " ") D Battery at G. 32. d. 2. 0. (" " ") The Brigade forms a sub group of left group of 1st D.A. It is attached for instruction and the following arrangements have been made. Batteries of 188 Bde are attached as follows. A 188 to 116 Batty B 188 " 51 " D 188 " 30 "	NWT

WAR DIARY or INTELLIGENCE SUMMARY

Army Form C. 2118

(Erase heading not required.)

Instructions regarding War Diaries and Intelligence Summaries are contained in F. S. Regs., Part II. and the Staff Manual respectively. Title Pages will be prepared in manuscript.

Place	Date	Hour	Summary of Events and Information	Remarks and references to Appendices
			(a) An experienced officer from the instructing battery will be attached to each of 188 Bde batteries until further orders to act as adviser to the OC.	
			(b) An officer from each 188 Battery will be attached to the instructing battery for duty.	
			(c) A proportion of NCOs and specialists of 188 Brigade batteries will be interchanged with the instructing batteries.	
			(d) Subalterns of 188 Bde FO for batteries will accompany the liaison officers of the left group batteries to Battalion HQ each night. On night of 14/5 inst A.188 & B.188 will send officers to left and right Battalion respectively. Afterwards each Batty will send to R & L Battalion alternately.	
			(e) As far as possible retaliation and offensive action on instructing battery fronts will be carried out by the 188 Brigade batteries.	
	15		Telephonic communication very poor. The Brigade using the left group system laid through a Central Exchange. A quiet day the Germans scarcely firing at all. Cloudy. Raining at intervals. Glass 29.9.	
	16		Great difficulty experienced with Telephonic communication. The amount of wire carried by Battalion is too little and the lines are taken by outgoing units very complicated the Battery's work which could easily made tidy. Visited by Genl Reed 4th D.A. who was much satisfied at the progress made by batteries in the last communication. Batteries fire on pillars and zone allotted to them as under.	
			"A" one gun on Trench Junction M4.c.7.1 B. one gun in red Junct M4.d.6½.4½ D. one gun in trench M6.c.1.4
			M4.c.4.1 " " " M5.c.½.6 " " " M5.c.8½
			M4.d.½.1 " " " M5.c.1.3½ " " " M5c3½.4
			" " " M10.d.9.9 " " " M6.c.2.9½ " " " M5.c.4.1
	16		Difficulty with Telephones still continues. A Battery Officer visits HQ daily of all Batteries and reports all Telephone system to HQ for an hour frees over the exchange than telephoning all communication. Battalion reports lines down. Not one alarmed no telephone communication.	
	17		Good progress made with Telephones. Batteries fire on pillars. Clear weather. Bar. 30.2. The signal officer	
				MWK

WARD DIARY
or
INTELLIGENCE SUMMARY
(Erase heading not required.)

Army Form C. 2118

Instructions regarding War Diaries and Intelligence Summaries are contained in F. S. Regs., Part II. and the Staff Manual respectively. Title Pages will be prepared in manuscript.

Place	Date	Hour	Summary of Events and Information	Remarks and references to Appendices
Le Brebis	18.		Quiet day. Batteries register. How[t] Batty well placed does not need to dig much deeper. But B + A Batteries need to dig	
"	19.	9.30 o'clock	Barometer 29.75 Thermometer 54. Quiet day. Very cold.	
"	20.	14.19 o'clock	Barometer 29.96 Thermometer 56. Quiet day cold	
"	21.	9 am	Barometer 29.96 rising. Thermometer 53. Cool day. Cloudy early morning with good light later till 16 o'clock when it became misty. Shelling S end of Double Crassier shelled 6 to 7 am. Dead man S Theodore	
"	22.	9 am	Barometer 29.95 rising. Thermometer 60. Morning very fine but hazy, making observation difficult, dull later. Hostile plane seen descending in direction of Lens after being under our anti aircraft fire. Shells seen noisy burst directed about at 11 h 3.6. Gas Alert on 5 pm.	
"	23.	9 am	Early mist but hazy. Very hot day. Stuffy. 9 am. Barometer 29.80 Thermometer 64. Makes up for a Thunder storm all day. Burst at 16 o'clock very heavy storm for 3/4 hour. Two Test Gas Alarms.	
				NWF

WAR DIARY or INTELLIGENCE SUMMARY

Army Form C. 2118

Instructions regarding War Diaries and Intelligence Summaries are contained in F. S. Regs., Part II. and the Staff Manual respectively. Title Pages will be prepared in manuscript.

(Erase heading not required.)

Place	Date	Hour	Summary of Events and Information	Remarks and references to Appendices
	24.		Barometer 29.8 Thermometer 60°. Observation conditions fair till 19.40 when heavy mist made observation impossible. Germans could be seen working in 2nd down from Signal box at M.11.b.2.9. Top of Pole 12 containing pulleys for mine shaft has been knocked down during the night. Enemy very busy erecting shelter from pine[?] behind the M.C. strong. Thermometer & Barometer taken with barometer at 9 o'clock am.	
	25.		Barometer 29.89 Thermometer 61 weather conditions [illegible] heavy mist no [illegible] made observation impossible. Barometer 29.77 Thermometer 69 [illegible] bright. Little wind. Observation conditions good.	
	27.		There is to be an Infantry attack on the 30th and followed the left group will be to give perfect. & requests for his purpose. Barometer 29.00 Thermometer 58 [illegible] Colonel & Capt. & gen. of the[?] Recruits & Right group of 47th D.A. to reconnoitre positions [illegible] the [illegible] Group H.Q. (Col [illegible]) at 9.30 a.m. Sheet 36 b.S.W. R21.C.88 All the positions they[?] from [illegible] built [illegible] by the French just had been heavy shelled. Like all French positions they are provided with good dug-outs but are not dug in for the guns. Best positions chosen are R.22.b.9.0 R.22.a.2.2 for 318 pdr Battery and R. 22.C.9.4 for Hors[?]	

1875 Wt. W593/826 1,000,000 4/15 J.B.C. & A. A.D.S.S./Forms/C. 2118.

WAR DIARY or INTELLIGENCE SUMMARY

Army Form C. 2118

Place	Date	Hour	Summary of Events and Information	Remarks and references to Appendices
	27 cont		Weather bad in the morning but improved during the day.	
	28.		Barometer 29.55 Thermometer 55 Poor weather. Batteries engaged in registering for attack on 30th. The plan of attack as partly disclosed by Col Sharpe at Left Group is as follows. Three feints at wire cutting one man into each. 1st Group to take point of triangle north of Carencey. All tactical orders go to Batteries from Left Group.	
	29th		Barometer 29.8 Thermometer 58 Weather fine. Colonel & Orderly Officer proceed to Aix Noulette to go to Lorette - Col Sharpe holds a conference to explain plans for 30th	
	30th		Barometer 29.75 Thermometer 59. A very quiet day preparatory for attack tonight	

C Holmes Wilson
Lt Col RFA
Comdg 183 Bde RFA

WAR DIARY or INTELLIGENCE SUMMARY

D Battery 188 Bde R.F.A.

Army Form C. 2118

Place	Date	Hour	Summary of Events and Information	Remarks and references to Appendices
DEEPCUT			The Battery was mobilised at DEEPCUT where the preliminary & subsequent training was carried out.	
FARNBOROUGH	4.6.16	10.15 AM	The Battery entrained at FARNBOROUGH by half Batteries. The first train leaving at 10.15 AM. & the second at 11.30 AM. On arrival at SOUTHAMPTON horses, guns & a proportion of officers & men were at once embarked on S.S. NORTH WESTERN MILLAR. The remainder of the officers & men were embarked on a smaller ship.	
HARVRE	5.6.16	1 PM	Crossing rough but horses did not suffer. Disembarked at HARVRE 2 P.M. The Battery collected & marched to Rest Camp No 5 where excellent accommodation was provided for men & horses.	
HARVRE	6.6.16	7.30 PM	Entrained for area of concentration for 40th Divn. One horse came down & broke his leg & had to be shot.	
BERGUETTE	7.6.16	5 PM	~~Disembarked &~~ Detrained and marched to billets in NEDON about 13 miles arrived 9.30 P.M. Billets comfortable, but horse lines very boggy owing to heavy rain.	
NEDON			In Billets at NEDON from 7-6-16 — 11-6-16	

WAR DIARY or INTELLIGENCE SUMMARY

D Battery 188 Bde R.F.A.

Army Form C. 2118

Place	Date	Hour	Summary of Events and Information	Remarks and references to Appendices
NEDON	11-6-16	9 AM	Left section marched to NOEUX-LES-MINES about 13 miles. Right section remained at NEDON under command of LT W.J. PRICE.	
NOEUX-LES-MINES	11-6-16	4 PM	Arrived and went into wagon line occupied by D/62 R.F.A. Guns were handed over to D/62 R.F.A. Staff & detachments marched to battery position of D/62 R.F.A. & took over their L.X. guns. The L.X. was under instruction from D/62 until 13-6-16 when the RX arrived from NEDON & completed the relief of D/62 who were withdrawn from the line same night.	
N. MAROC	14-6-16		The Battery now came under the instruction of the O.C. 30th Battery R.F.A. The battery position was at M26 2½.10 and the O.P at M36 0.10 Reference LENS 36C.SW1 Edition 7A Scale 1 in 10,000. The Zone allotted was from M4C 6½.8 to M6C 8½.8½. The guns taken over were very old & their shooting was very inaccurate. The gun pits were	

WAR DIARY or INTELLIGENCE SUMMARY

D Battery 188 Bde R.F.A.

Army Form C. 2118

Place	Date	Hour	Summary of Events and Information	Remarks and references to Appendices
			fairly strong but required a lot of additions & improvements. Section Commanders & detachments worked with a will at their pits, producing excellent results. The G.O.C 40th Divn. & the GOC, R.A. both expressed their great satisfaction with the work performed.

The wagon line during this period had been three times shifted but was finally established at K 24 b 10.6 Reference FRANCE Sheet 36 B 3rd Edition 1 in 40,000. The weather was very bad, rain falling continuously. The Officer in charge of the Wagon line 2/LT H.T.P. MOORE had many difficulties to overcome in order to provide cover for men and harness. By 28-6-16 when he handed over to LT W.2 PRICE he had accomplished this quite successfully. He was very ably assisted by B.S.M. HEATH and especially by Farrier Sgt FREEMAN. | |

WAR DIARY

Army Form C. 2118

D Battery 188 Brigade R.F.A.

Place	Date	Hour	Summary of Events and Information	Remarks and references to Appendices
N. MAROC	30-6-16	9.10 P.M.	The G.O.C. R.A. 40th Divn visited the wagon line several times during this period. In a letter to the O.C. Brigade he described the wagon line of D/188 as "the only bright-spot" amongst the wagon lines of the Brigade. A minor operation was carried out on the night June 30th. It was proposed to take possession of & hold the W. face of The Triangle M4d 8.4 — M5c 2.9. For this purpose the whole of the system of trenches about the Triangle was bombarded for 7 minutes & 4 mines were exploded. The particular portion allotted to the Battery was the Hun 3rd Line Trench M5c 1.3 — M5c 2.5½. At 9.10 P.M. the bombardment commenced	

WAR DIARY or INTELLIGENCE SUMMARY

D Battery 188 Brigade RFA

Army Form C. 2118

Place	Date	Hour	Summary of Events and Information	Remarks and references to Appendices
	During June		and at 9.17 PM the mines were exploded & batteries on the front line lifted. The assaulting columns were seen to enter the German front line without any difficulty. They afterwards, however, came under enfilade machine gun fire & had to withdraw to their original position. The Battery fired one round from each gun every 15 secs for 10 minutes & kept this rate up without any difficulty, which is very satisfactory for unseasoned gunners. 1 NCO & 1 GR evacuated through sickness & struck off strength. 3 horses struck off. 6 men posted from 185 Bde RFA.	

WAR DIARY or INTELLIGENCE SUMMARY

D Battery 188 Bde R.F.A.

Place	Date	Hour	Summary of Events and Information	Remarks and references to Appendices
	30-6-16.		11 men sent on Trench Mortar Courses during June. I consider that N.C.O's & Men for Trench Mortar Batteries should be obtained from Home & that newly formed units should not be weakened by withdrawing their personnel for Trench Mortars immediately after arrival in this country. This particularly applies to Officers & Senior N.C.O's. M Percival CAPT. R.F.A. COMDG. D/188TH BRIGADE, R.F.A.	

40 / July

188 R.F.A.

Vol 2

CONFIDENTIAL

War Diary
of
188th Brigade R.F.A. (1st Group 40th D.A.)

from 1st July 1916 to 31st July 1916.

(Volume I.)

A Holmes à Court
Lt. Col. Commdg.
188th Brigade R.F.A. 1st Group 40 D.A.

WAR DIARY or INTELLIGENCE SUMMARY

Army Form C. 2118

Instructions regarding War Diaries and Intelligence Summaries are contained in F. S. Regs., Part II. and the Staff Manual respectively. Title Pages will be prepared in manuscript.

(Erase heading not required.)

Place	Date	Hour	Summary of Events and Information	Remarks and references to Appendices
	1st		The attack last night passed off without a hitch in so far as the Artillery fire was concerned. The following reports received from the Infantry. (1) that the raid was successful and that our men gained the enemy trenches unopposed (2) that after some hours they were subjected however to enfilade fire from a concealed machine gun in the north side of Crassier. Result as far as ascertaining out the batteries NIL. Strategical result is keeping the Germans busy & unable to remove troops from this front of course unknown to lower commanders.	
	2nd		A Quiet day. Orders arrive late that the 40th D.A. is to take over from the 1st Division. The 40th D.A. to be divided into two Groups. Right Group under Lt Col Gold composed of 1 gun D 155, "D" & "C" 185 & 178 Brigade. Left Group composed of 188 Brigade, A B & C Batteries of 181 Brigade A Battery & three guns of D Battery 185 Brigade.	
	3rd		The Left Group 40th Div. began to take over from left group 1st Div. night of 3/4. The matter is very complicated as the incoming batteries are distributed throughout the 15 & 66 Divs, many of them being split up and having guns all over the place. Half batteries are to come in at a time. Guns taken over from 1st Division as they are in pits with small stores complete.	

WAR DIARY
or
INTELLIGENCE SUMMARY
(Erase heading not required.)

Army Form C. 2118

Instructions regarding War Diaries and Intelligence Summaries are contained in F. S. Regs., Part II. and the Staff Manual respectively. Title Pages will be prepared in manuscript.

Place	Date	Hour	Summary of Events and Information	Remarks and references to Appendices
	4th		Half relief completed at 3.15 am this morning. Bde H.Q. moves into house occupied by [illegible] Left Group. [illegible] the MINE BUILDING at LES BREBIS L35a 5.3. Sheet 36 NE.	
	6th		The remaining half of batteries arrive & relief completed at 1.20 am. Batteries are now arranged as follows:—	
			(1) 188 Bde — A. stays in its present position at G 31 a 2.8	
			[illegible] B. " " " " " " G 26 c 2.2	
			C. relieves the 96th Bty at G 32 c 15.1	
			D. relieves the 30th Bty at M 2 d 15.6	
			(2) 10[?] Bde A. relieves 115th Bty at G 33 a 8.6	
			B. relieves 96th Bty at G a[?] d 2.1	
			C. relieves 59th Bty at M 1 d 9.8	
			(3) 10[?] Bde A. relieves detachment of 96th Bty with 2 guns at Fosse 7. G 29 d 2.8	
			B.(How) Line guns " " " at G 30 d 1.9	
			[illegible] at G 35 b 7.7	
			D. relieves one howt at Cité[?] M 14 c 3.6	
			How[?] at [illegible] G 35 d 6.9	
			How[?] at [illegible] M 2 d 15.6	
			Note. D 100 [illegible] 2 guns in his [illegible] one of him from D185[?] [illegible] C 10[?] [illegible] 1 gun and 1 howt at CAYONNE.	

WAR DIARY or INTELLIGENCE SUMMARY

Army Form C. 2118

Instructions regarding War Diaries and Intelligence Summaries are contained in F. S. Regs., Part II. and the Staff Manual respectively. Title Pages will be prepared in manuscript.

(Erase heading not required.)

Place	Date	Hour	Summary of Events and Information	Remarks and references to Appendices
	6th		181 Bde H.Q. established at old 188 Bde H.Q. at	
	7th		The Group is being worked on the lines left by the old Group until fresh registration is carried out and new schemes of concentration devised. Barometer 29.7 A quiet day.	
	8th		Barometer 29.6 Thermometer 59½ at 9 o'clock. Observation conditions good. Quiet day.	
	9th		Barometer 29.5 Thermometer 64 at 10 o'clock. Last night gas alarm - by Infantry who actually wore their helmets for ½ an hour. Otherwise a very quiet night.	
	10th		Barometer 29.6 Thermometer 59½ at 9 o'clock. A very quiet day. Situation normal.	
	11th		Barometer 29.06 Thermometer 59 at 9 o'clock. 1 & 2 this morning B188 & B189 fired a large number of rounds in cooperation with 16th Division on small attack for the purpose of raiding the enemy's trenches.	
	12th		Barometer 29.96 Thermometer 59.5 at 9 o'clock. Quiet day.	
	13th		Barometer 30 Thermom: 60.5 at 9 o'clock. A quiet day.	
	14th		Barometer 30.01 Thermom: 61.5 at 9 o'clock. A very quiet day.	

WAR DIARY
or
INTELLIGENCE SUMMARY
(Erase heading not required.)

Army Form C. 2118

Instructions regarding War Diaries and Intelligence Summaries are contained in F. S. Regs., Part II. and the Staff Manual respectively. Title Pages will be prepared in manuscript.

Place	Date	Hour	Summary of Events and Information	Remarks and references to Appendices
			Barometer 30.2 Thermometer 60°s at noon. During the past fortnight the following in first Army have been registered.	
			A.100 M.5.c.20.60 and again from line towards M.5.c.90.30.	
			A.101 M.5.c.90.70	
			M.5.a.30.30	
			M.5.d.75.80	
			M.5.d.90.40	
			A.158 M.5.c.90.22 C.101 M.10.c.10.40	
			M.5.c.75.47 M.10.c.20.70	
			M.5.c.70.00 M.10.c.08.55	
			M.5.c.85.72 M.10.c.50.91	
			A.125 M.5.d.80.07	
			M.5.d.96.30 D.158 M.10.c.10.40	
			M.5.a.90.30 M.10.a.60.60	
			M.5.c.09.87 M.4.c.85.40	
			M.5.c.90.22	
			C.100 M.10.a.40.40 M.5.d.90.50	
			M.10.a.60.40	
			M.10.a.60.60	
			M.10.a.00.00	
			M.4.c.60.08	
			M.4.a.85.40	
			M.4.c.90.40	
			Today C.101 leaves the Group and goes to the North of Loos Salient where another Group is being formed to join the 8th Division.	

1875 Wt. W593/826 1,000,000 4/15 J.B.C. & A. A.D.S.S./Forms/C. 2118.

WAR DIARY or INTELLIGENCE SUMMARY

(Erase heading not required.)

Army Form C. 2118

Instructions regarding War Diaries and Intelligence Summaries are contained in F. S. Regs., Part II. and the Staff Manual respectively. Title Pages will be prepared in manuscript.

Place	Date	Hour	Summary of Events and Information	Remarks and references to Appendices
			Three guns of B181 move into posn of C181. B goes away an B controls again the new gun which has been at Calonne to hitherto controlled by C181. The following officers are posted to this Brigade as from the 12 inst. Temp'y 2nd Lt A. Morgan RFA to A188 Temp'y 2nd Lt T.S. Hancock RFA to B188 — this officer had been in this Brigade at Dupaw but left behind. Temp'y 2nd Lt H.P. Longton RFA to C 188 Temp'y 2nd Lt C.D. Robertson RFA to D188	
	16th	9 o'clock	Barometer 30.01 Thermometer 61.5. A quiet dull day. Activity of Enemy very much less than usual.	
	17th		Barometer 30.01 Thermometer 61. Another very quiet day. Much less Artillery fire than usual. Observation conditions very bad.	
	18th	9 o'clock	Barometer 29.88 Thermometer 61.5. Observation conditions very bad a very quiet day on both sides.	
	19th		Wire cutting operations carried out by A181, C188, B188, B181. A181 cuts two feint gaps in W face of Triangle. M.4.d 84. & M 8 c 08. C188 cuts two gaps at M 4 c 90.34 and M 10 a 70.93 B188 cuts one gap at M 4 c 75.35. B181 two gaps at M 10 c 20.70 M 9 d 92.30	A.Wilkin

1875 Wt. W593/826 1,000,000 4/15 J.B.C. & A. A.D.S.S./Forms/C. 2118.

Instructions regarding War Diaries and Intelligence Summaries are contained in F. S. Regs., Part II. and the Staff Manual respectively. Title Pages will be prepared in manuscript.

WAR DIARY
or
INTELLIGENCE SUMMARY
(Erase heading not required.)

Army Form C. 2118

Place	Date	Hour	Summary of Events and Information	Remarks and references to Appendices
			Allowance of ammunition 200 rounds to each of the main gaps i.e. the gaps to be cut by Major [illegible]'s Battery C 188 & the gaps to be cut by Major Coppell's Battery B 175 and 100 rounds each to the gaps cut by Major Sinclair A 188 & Capt Rogers A 181. A [illegible] [illegible] except for the wire cutting.	
			Barometer 29.8 Thermometer 60.5. Infantry patrols report that wire was not properly cut so the cutting had to continue today and they are to go out again to look at it tonight; Major [illegible] used another 200 rounds. Major Coppell another 250 & Capt Rogers 150 rounds Major Sinclair 50 rounds. [illegible] [illegible] [illegible] [illegible] [illegible] Infantry [illegible] [illegible] [illegible] result of wire cutting. Zero time 10.30. 0.5 0.8 bombardment of [illegible] [illegible]	
			Lift to intense bombardment on enemy front line	
			C 188 Bde M4 c 90.35 to M4 c 75.20	
			A 188 M4 c 75.20 to M10 a 65.90	
			B 188 M10 a 65.95 to M10 a 65.75	
			A 188 2pm M10 a 60.95 to	
			A 181 6pm M10 a 70.60 to	
			at Zero 18 Batteries lift and establish Barrage 125 yards [illegible] [illegible] [illegible]	
			then at Zero 10 lift again and establish Barrage as follows:–	

[illegible signature]

1875 Wt. W593/826 1,000,000 4/15 J.B.C. & A. A.D.S.S./Forms/C. 2118.

WAR DIARY or INTELLIGENCE SUMMARY

Place	Date	Hour	Summary of Events and Information	Remarks and references to Appendices
			Barrage C188 Pozs 2guns M4d 34.20 2guns M4d 25.11	
			B178 2 guns M4d 85.08 2 guns M10b 32.87 1 gun M10b 35.55	
			A188 2 guns M10a 70.62 " " M10a 95.63	
			B188 1 gun M4d 55.08 1 gun M10b 32.87 1 gun M10a 95.63 2 gun M10b 27.75	
			A181 1 gun M10a 70.62	
			D188 M10a 70.62 M10b 20.55 M10b 32.87 M4d 55.08 M4d 25.11	
			A155 M10a 70.60 M10a 99.60 M10b 20.55	

This barrage was to have lasted 45 minutes or such shorter time as to allow our Infantry raiding parties who were to enter 3 gaps at M4c 90.34, M4c 75.35, M10a 70.93. The raiding party at North gap were demoralised by blowing up of our mines under the Crater, this party came back in 10 mins with a few men wounded. Centre gap party did not get beyond the wire. South gap party who lost their officer got scattered did not get to enemy trench and were not all back till 12.25. Artillery fire slackened at 11.35. The object of the trench operation was to get a prisoner dead or alive. This was effected quite by chance as a German ran across to our line premeditately to give himself up and was shot by our Infantry.

Barometer 30. Thermometer 29.2. A quiet day.

21st

WAR DIARY or INTELLIGENCE SUMMARY

Army Form C. 2118

Place	Date	Hour	Summary of Events and Information	Remarks and references to Appendices
	22?		Baranche 31/7 Received diary ?? — A very quiet day. a little register at ?? by our guns. no reply from the enemy.	
	28?		Baranche 20.08 The nominal GO another very quiet day. a scarcely any firing on either side. Rearrangement of 4th Division. Division take over ?? line — left group covers the left Brigade from H.31.b.25.30 to point of Double Crassier. Left group consist of: A 181 Bde A 188 Bde D 185 Bde (2 Hrs) B 182 Bde C 188 Bde D 188 Bde and a sub group under Col Robertson of 181 Bde consisting of: C 181 Bde D 181 Bde C 185 Bde A 188 Bde Les Brisson (line held by left group) supports infantry as follows: Right Battalion — End of Crassier to M5.d 40.95 — C 188 Bde & A 188 Bde. Centre " — M5.d 40.95 to M.6.6 30.60 — B 188 Bde & A 181 Bde. Left Battalion — M.6.6 30.60 to H.31.a 65.20 — A 188 C 181 & C 185.	

WAR DIARY or INTELLIGENCE SUMMARY

Army Form C. 2118

(Erase heading not required.)

Place	Date	Hour	Summary of Events and Information	Remarks and references to Appendices
	23rd		Normal Zones of Observation to be covered and watched by Batteries allotted as follows.	
			A. 188 Bde H 31 b 26. 25 to H 31 c 95. 15	
			C 185 H 31 c 95. 15 to N 1 a 20. 60	
			C 181 N 1 a 20. 60 to M 6 b 50. 05	
			A 181 M 6 b 50. 05 to M 6 c 25. 45	
			B 188 M 6 c 25. 45 to M 5 d 35. 30	
			A 185 M 5 d 35. 30 to M 5 c 30. 70	
			C 188 M 5 c 30. 70 to M 4 c 85. 60	
			Two How. Batteries cover the whole front.	
			The group loses Capt Rogers and B 181 which goes to Right Group. The new Batteries take positions as follows.	
			D 181 M 2 d. 2. 0	
			C 181 G 22 d 22. 12	
			C 185 G 26 d 50. 20	
			A 188 moves from his old position G 31 a 8. 8 to a new position G 26 d 80. 70.	
			Otherwise balance of old Group remain unchanged.	
	24th		Barometer 30. 08. Thermometer 59. Enemy shows more activity with T.M.s & our fire is directed to keep him down.	

Place	Date	Hour	Summary of Events and Information	Remarks and references to Appendices
	25th		Bar: 30.04 Ther 57.5. Observation conditions good. Enemy shelled our trenches round HARTS & HARRISONS Craters with T.M's. Our retaliation with artillery was very successful the enemy only carrying when our T.M's got to work in late afternoon. Otherwise all quiet.	
	26th		Bar. 30.04 Ther 58. Operations confined to registration by batteries of points for new concentrations schemes & to concentration chiefly in the neighbourhood of HARRISONS CRATER. No retaliation for T.M activity on the front of this enemy.	
	27th		Bar 30.04 Ther 57. A very quiet day much less fog. We continued registration and did not have to retaliate till 19 o'clock when enemy started T.M's on HARRISONS Crater. Observation conditions poor.	
	28th		Bar 30.08 Ther 59. Except for T.M. activity on the enemy front round HARRISONS Crater during afternoon. Enemy shelled No 15X for about 2 hours from 16 to 18 o'clock. No harm done. At 21.40 enemy began shelling the level crossing on BREBIS MAROC Road and all down the road with 4.2's. Infantry called for retaliation & a concentration was fired on M 5c on account of shelling on front line opposite triangle. The enemy bombardment probably resulted of a scare on their part as a fresh Battalion went up into the line and was observed by enemy Sausages. They probably thought we would attack.	

1875 Wt. W593/826 1,000,000 4/15 J.B.C. & A. A.D.S.S./Forms/C. 2118.

WAR DIARY or INTELLIGENCE SUMMARY

Army Form C. 2118

Place	Date	Hour	Summary of Events and Information	Remarks and references to Appendices
	29th		Bar 30.05. Ther 62. A very quiet day. Less hostile mortar activity. C.181 changes one section from G.22.d.22.12 to M.2.b.3.6.	
	30th		Bar 30.05 Ther 63. A quiet day. Misty till 1 oclock. Less mortar activity. Our firing consisted of one concerted retaliation and registration. C.181 completes move to new position M.2.b.3.6.	
	31st		Bar 30.08 Ther 69 Very much quieter. Hun using his mortars much less. A concentration fired owing to enemy mortar bombs dropping in Loos at midday, otherwise all quite quiet.	

Vol 3

Confidential
─────────
War Diary
of
188th Brigade R.F.A.
from August — August 31st 1916
(Volume I)

31/8/16.

C H Liddell
LIEUT.-COL., R.F.A.
COMMANDING 188TH BRIGADE, R.F.A

WAR DIARY or INTELLIGENCE SUMMARY

Army Form C. 2118

Place	Date	Hour	Summary of Events and Information	Remarks and references to Appendices
	1st August		A very Quiet day. Bar: 30.09 Ther: 68.	
	2nd		Another quiet day Bar 30.12 Ther. 67. Operations confined to retaliation behind Harrisons Crater & on the TRIANGLE this latter retaliation joined in by the Heavies. An anti aircraft shell fell in garden next door to H.Q.	
	3rd August		The day quiet. Bar 31.07 Ther 68. At 12.15 the Infantry made a raid on the German Trenches just souter of Loos Crassier. A 181. C 181. C 185. C 188 supported the attack. Bombardment for 5 minutes at Rate of fire of Battery Fire 3 seconds. then lift to support trenches for 39 minutes at average of Battery Fire 3 seconds. The attack was not successful as the Infantry were insufficiently supplied with Trench Ladders. The Bombardment and Barrage went off without a hitch. Enemy made little or no reply.	
	4th August		Bar 31.06 Ther 64. A very quiet day - usual Mortar activity, but hardly any infantry fire. A very lively night. 16th Division carrying out a raid with big Bombardment.	
	5. August		Bar 31.07 Ther 62. Enemy opened fire on C 181 at G.22.d.22.12. about 30 rounds of 4.2's and 5.9's. 5 direct hits one into gun pit used by Major Rowe as an office. Killed one man and dangerously wounded Major Rowe and one Corporal. In afternoon Enemy shelled B 188 G. 26. c. 2. 2. wounding two gunners. Otherwise a very quiet day. Here note that Major Leggett left B 188 on 24th July evacuated with German Measles we hear today that he has died in No 7 Genl Hospital at Boulogne this should have been entered up under date. His place as O.C. B 188 taken by Lt McGillewie late of B Bty 178th Bde R.F.A. posted 26th July.	

MW

WAR DIARY or INTELLIGENCE SUMMARY

Army Form C. 2118

Instructions regarding War Diaries and Intelligence Summaries are contained in F. S. Regs., Part II. and the Staff Manual respectively. Title Pages will be prepared in manuscript.

(Erase heading not required.)

Place	Date	Hour	Summary of Events and Information	Remarks and references to Appendices
	6th Aug.		Bar 30.14 Ther 58. The enemy artillery quieter than usual but T.M's very much more active. Our artillery activity confined to retaliation at urgent request of the Infantry. A great deal of aerial activity. Enemy shelled C188 with 4.2's at 11.00 to 11.40 a.m. Direct hit on gun pit but no damage done. Enemy shelled A188 various other. OC A/188 wires reports that shells fired at his position yesterday were partly 4.2's and partly 5.9's. C185 also shelled with 4.2's	
	7th Aug		Bar 30.1 Ther 58. Artillery fire both enemy & ourselves insignificant, but Trench Mortar activity unprecedented. Enemy began shortly and continued all day. Enemy very much harassed also retaliation for enemy shells and our own rifle fire most effective against the mortars for retaliation. The retaliation we have had on when fire was most effective were the mortars to [illegible]. Enemy fired a few accurate shots on C185 & A188	
	8th Aug.		Bar [illegible] Ther 58. A very quiet day — very little artillery fire. Mortars much quieter than usual except for one burst of fire in the afternoon for which a heavy retaliation was dealt out. Tonight and tomorrow the 4th Division front & Corps change of front takes over a [illegible] the 1st Division, and the Left and Right Groups are reconstituted. Are now exactly as they were at the date, away from the 1st Divl. except that the Lone Howt. at Calonne is now under Right Group but keeps on its old sights same as Tunnel to Cransiez. This becomes the following changes of Batteries. A186 goes to its old position at T.36.a.80.80. C181 moves to its old position at M.1.d.90.80 and Buffshir lone gun at CALLONNE ironstone, [illegible] by B.181. B.181 stays in its old position but comes back under the control of Left Group from Right Group. D181 goes to the Heavy Counter Groups and C185 to the Right Group.	

1875 Wt. W593/826 1,000,000 4/15 J.B.C. & A. A.D.S.S./Forms/C. 2118.

Place	Date	Hour	Summary of Events and Information	Remarks and references to Appendices
	9th		Bar 30.09 Ther 68. A very quiet day from artillery point of view. Enemy used more rifle grenades than usual otherwise the day was particularly quiet.	
	10th		Bar. 30.04 Ther 62. Our artillery very quiet as also enemy day spent in registration. The enemy hit just below loophole in Capt Rogers's B188's OP at M.36.18. With a 77. No damage done & reckoned to be a chance shot. The Regtl S.M. Macdonald obtain a commission was sent and is attached to B178 for training.	
	11th		Bar. 30. Ther 60. Another very quiet day. Rather misty until the evening. The enemy fired very little. Major Vickery C188 spent 50 rounds each on the two gaps cut in previous mortar operations at M 10.a 60.90 and M 4 d 63.09. These gaps are being cut to mark our wire just south by the left group.	
	12th		Bar 29.98. Ther 62. A very Quiet Day. Major Vickery shot 76 more rounds into the two gaps made yesterday. Lt Rogers B181. registered with 50 rounds 5 points for a false Barrage. At night 119th Infantry made a raid. Capt Rogers B181 fired 80 rounds on his Barrage points. Capt Vickery Von its just at zero hour of his raid thinking they saw white rockets started firing an S.O.S. but was stopped in 5 minutes. The raid in front of the Right Group successful thro' the personal gallantry of Capt Richard who picked up a Hun and carried him to his own wounded.	
	13th		Bar 29.9. Ther 63. Another Quiet day the enemy was noticeably less active here known at Rvs.	AWE

.

WAR DIARY
or
INTELLIGENCE SUMMARY

(Erase heading not required.)

Army Form C. 2118

Instructions regarding War Diaries and Intelligence Summaries are contained in F. S. Regs., Part II. and the Staff Manual respectively. Title Pages will be prepared in manuscript.

Place	Date	Hour	Summary of Events and Information	Remarks and references to Appendices
14th			Bar. 29.75 Ther. 61. A quiet day. [illegible handwriting regarding weather conditions, enemy activity below normal, our artillery quiet except for fact that each Battery has got 32 rounds for unit and purposes.]	
15th			[illegible] Ther 62. Enemy Artillery very active. Started by shelling MARSC at 8.15. [long handwritten entry, largely illegible, mentioning shelling with intensity all day, shells, A/S, direction of WARGATES, no damage done, rebuild, enemy put about 35 4.2" into the British front line, etc.]	
16th			Bar 29.7 Ther 63. A very quiet day. Activity of all sorts far below normal. A few hostile shells fell in and about FOSSE 7. Two shrieks [?] of shrapnel fell [illegible]	

1875 Wt. W593/826 1,000,000 4/15 J.B.C. & A. A.D.S.S./Forms/C. 2118.

WAR DIARY or INTELLIGENCE SUMMARY

Army Form C. 2118

(Erase heading not required.)

Place	Date	Hour	Summary of Events and Information	Remarks and references to Appendices
	17th		Bar 29.63 Therm 62. Another very quiet day. All actions below normal.	
	18th		Bar. 29.5. Therm 59. A very quiet day scarcely any fire on our front but a big Mortar Show from Bosch in Right Group and considerable activity to our left on 16th Divn front.	
	19th		Bar 29.20 Thermometer 60. All very quiet in this sector. Practically no mortar fire and very little mortar activity. A small aim rifle sprung by enemy at southern end of Beaver Crossing. Very little movement among them in the enemy trenches.	
	20th		Bar. 29.82 Thermometer 60. Another quiet day. Very little activity of any kind. The 77's were fired at O.P. situated on B122 & B121. One shell burst in door of telephone dug-out wounding 3 telephonists, one severely. Communication was re-established at alternative O.P.	
	21st		Bar. 29.85. Thermometer 58. All quite quiet. A sizeable explosion caused by our fire in trenches at Mod ge.30. Observation conditions in morning bad, good later.	
	22nd		Bar. 29.94 Ther 60. Another eventless quiet day. In the evening B121 & B121 helped the 16th Divn Right Group with fire from a section each on following Barrage Points for 5 min M15 d&2.75 — M15 b 97.02. 2nd Lt Rutler found evacuated sick from symptoms shewing continued result of shell shock experienced some time back before going a sick leave to England a few days back.	
	23rd		Bar. 29.95 Ther 57. A very quiet day. 2nd Lt I.H. Lewis posted from D 188 Bde to C 188 Bde R.F.A.	

WAR DIARY or INTELLIGENCE SUMMARY

Army Form C. 2118

(Erase heading not required.)

Place	Date	Hour	Summary of Events and Information	Remarks and references to Appendices
	24th		Bar. 29.84 Ther 61. A very quiet day.	
	25th		Bar. 30.78 Ther 62. Att my quiet enemy fire, little activity on front about the Tihes. 2nd Lt. Walker posted from B/159 Bde to D/175 Bde.	
	26th		Bar. 29.5 Ther 60. A very quiet day. At end of m/on the artillery brought [?] demonstration of artillery [?] took place [?] our [?] on 11th Division going out on our left and our [?] our [?] Batty [?] 4th [?] [?] [?] signal to H 25.c.8 inclusive. Four Artillery Groups were formed. (a) Callinan Group. Lt Col Jim, 179 Bde + 180 Bde less A/180, one 8" How one 9.2" over all Right [?] front. [?] Group Lt Col [?] 160 Bde + 158 [?] [?] over the left front. [?] Group C/R 181 Bde [?] three [?] how one How M85 [?] Group Lt Col [?] A/180 Bde + [?] Bde [?] How over [?] These two groups over at 1st Div front. Left group loc + hours for Capt Perceval, position in [?] and Major [?] Major [?] Capt [?] + Capt Rogers all leave the group [?] positions remain the same.	AWT

WAR DIARY or INTELLIGENCE SUMMARY

Army Form C. 2118

(Erase heading not required.)

Place	Date	Hour	Summary of Events and Information	Remarks and references to Appendices
	27th		Bar 29.6 Ther 61. A very quiet day & most marked absence of firing and of movement by the enemy. Lts W.E. Pendleton and T.L. Hancock are posted to 8th Division and proceed to join.	
	28th		Bar 29.59 Ther 62. All very quiet.	
	29th		Bar 29.55 Ther 61. Very bad weather - Tremendous Thunderstorm with Torrential Rain. No firing possible. Enemy also quite silent.	
	30th		Bar 29.18 Ther 60. Another day of shocking weather very quiet on both sides. Reliefs commence for formation of New Right group. Old right group area is later over by 63rd Div. Area now held by Loos group becomes New Left group 47th Div. Area held by us as Maroc group becomes Right group. Maroc group is reinforced by 6 guns to form new Right group. This change is made concurrently with reorganization of 188 Bde into a Brigade of two 6 gun Batteries about then of 18 pdr & two 4 gun Batteries of 4.5 Hows. Concurrently 181 & 178 Bdes become Bdes of 3 6 gun 18 Pdr Batteries & 1 Batty of 4.5 Hows. For the purpose of this reorganization of Divn Artillery, 185 Bde is broken up and the following rearrangements are made as far as 188 Bde is concerned.	

WAR DIARY
or
INTELLIGENCE SUMMARY
(Erase heading not required.)

Army Form C. 2118

Instructions regarding War Diaries and Intelligence Summaries are contained in F. S. Regs., Part II. and the Staff Manual respectively. Title Pages will be prepared in manuscript.

Place	Date	Hour	Summary of Events and Information	Remarks and references to Appendices

	30th Aug		C/188 Bde is split up. Left section C/188 goes to A/188 making A/188 a 6 gun Battery. Right section C/188 goes " B/188 " B/188 " " " D/185 Bde comes over to 188 Bde & becomes new C/188 Bde. The following change of Personnel takes place.
			
			__A/188 Bde.__ Capt D.C. Buchan from C/188 to A/188 to command A/188
			__B/188 Bde.__ Major C.E. Vichey DSO " C/188 to B/188 " " B/188
			        Lt F.P. Layton " C/188 to B/188
			        Lt C.D. Rutherford " C/188 to B/188
			        Lt J.H. Morris " C/188 to B/188
			        Lt H.B. Oldfield " C/188 to A/188
			        2/Lt H.S. Coates " C/188 to C/178
			
			__C/188 Bd.__ D Bty 185 becomes C/188 as under
			        Major G.W. Hole & command
			        Lt W Campbell
			        2/Lt A.E. Knoe
			        2/Lt A.G. Sharp.
			        2/Lt R.G. Ord.
				Nil

WAR DIARY or INTELLIGENCE SUMMARY

Place	Date	Hour	Summary of Events and Information	Remarks and references to Appendices
	30th August		The above changes come into force as from 1st Sept. inclusive. The formation of New Right Group under Lt Col Wilson is completed by charge of section of C178 with section of A188 already at Lone Tree position. Right Group now is situated as follows.	

A188 — 6 guns
    4 at Old A188 position   at L 36 a 80.85
    2 guns at position lately occupied by B188 at M 1 d 85.85

B188 — 6 guns
    4 at Old C188 position   at G 32 c 20.15
    2 at position lately occupied by B188 at G 31 d 30.15

D188 — 4 How's at position now occupied   at M 1 b 50.20

A178 — 6 guns
    4 guns at position now occupied by B188 Bde at G 26 c 20.30
    2 guns in adjoining position once occupied by 57 H.Bty at G 26 c 20.20
    2 guns at position at Lone Tree vacated by A188 at G 22 d 20.85

C178
D178 — 1 How. at Loos in its present position at G 35.b 00.60

Place	Date	Hour	Summary of Events and Information	Remarks and references to Appendices
	30th Aug (cont)		To effect this change in group & Brigade the following reliefs take place tonight, & are completed by 11 p.m. 1 section of C.178 changes with one section of A.185 at Lone Tree. 1 section of B.188 goes to man 2 guns handed over by A.178 to Major Vichez new B.188. 1 section of A.178 goes to present (old) B.188 to man guns vacated by the section going over to Major Vichez.	
	31st Aug.		Relief of group completed. Now constitutes Right Group 40th D.A. 11 p.m. A.178 puts 2 guns into position at M.1.d.85-85 for A Battery & these guns are manned by section from C.188 now split up and disolved. A.178 puts 2 guns into 57th Bty position at G.26.C.20.20. and mans them and two guns left by B.188. A.178 then has 6 guns manned. Remary section of B.188 goes across to new position at G.32.C.20.15. A. B.188 & A.178 have now become 6 gun batteries. Major Vichez controls the two guns of C.178 (Capt Noakes) at Lone Tree G.22.d.20.85. Start of 1st September. New Right Group as above. New Brigade Organization as above.	MvK

Vol 4

CONFIDENTIAL

WAR DIARY

of

125th Bde R.F.A.

from 1st Sept 1916 to 30th Sept 1916

Volume I

Chamberlain
Commanding
125th Bde. R.F.A.

WAR DIARY or INTELLIGENCE SUMMARY

Army Form C. 2118

Place	Date	Hour	Summary of Events and Information	Remarks and references to Appendices
	1st Sept	9 a.m.	Bar 29. Ther 60. New Right Group and Newly reorganized Brigade in being. A very quiet day almost total silence on the enemy's part both with mortars and guns and practically no movement seen.	
	1st Sept		Bar 30. [crossed out] MWF	
	2nd Sept		Bar 29.9. Ther 61. Everything very quiet on our front practically no firing from enemy. We are registering our new targets consequent on re-grouping. A mine has been sunk at Seaforth Craters and is about ready for action. It appears that the enemy have also got a mine here and it is a race which will go up first — great care is being taken to have all batteries of Left Group and such of ours as can support them ready to form a barrage immediately the mine goes up whether ours or the enemy's.	
	3rd Sept		Bar 30.09 Ther 62. A very quiet day. We hear at 11 a.m. that we are late and it is the enemy who will explode the mine some time during the next 12 hours. Vigilance is consequently redoubled. Mine exploded at 8.11. Artillery Barrage established at once and maintained for over an hour during which time we hear that the Huns are in our front line, then that they have been put out and bombing parties are fighting in No Man's Land. All this is fiction, as it transpires, No Huns entered our front line our bombing parties only met each other and an officer who penetrated into the enemy lines found them absolutely empty.	MWF

Place	Date	Hour	Summary of Events and Information	Remarks and references to Appendices
	4th Sept		Barometer 29.85 Therm. 64. A quiet day, bad weather, little regularity. The enemy almost entirely silent. There is a very noticeable quietness. Hardly a hostile gun has gone off for a week and even their T.M's are silent. The 63rd Division on our right had a small bombardment of the enemy. Billets between 8 & 9 pm heavier and Divisional Artillery, but not our absolutely no reply whatever.	
	5th Sept		Bar 29.71. Ther 60. .... Actually still a very quiet day.	
	6th Sept		Bar 29.70 Ther 58. Capt Perceval of B Battery gave 100 rounds B.X to knock out trench M9d 22.20 — M9c 90.25. He seemed good shoots getting a direct return at 70% over the trench. The day very quiet, no hostile artillery fire except when about to see a few rounds to not divert on Capt Perceval's shoot.	
	7th Sept		Bar 30. Ther 58. A quiet day and bright. Huns seem to be merely keeping watch.	
	8th Sept		Bar 30.05 Ther 58. Another quiet day so far as hostile fire is concerned. Their T.M.s did not cut up M10a + M9d. Capt Gray of B.... observing for the purpose of putting our artillery fire if the enemy retaliated on our front or supplies lines, which retaliation. This is unnecessary.	

WAR DIARY or INTELLIGENCE SUMMARY

Army Form C. 2118

(Erase heading not required.)

Place	Date	Hour	Summary of Events and Information	Remarks and references to Appendices
	9.9.16		Bar 30.16. Ther 58. Enemy a little more active than lately with a few 4.2's & 5.9's. Probably the result of our Mortar fire. Observation conditions poor in the morning improving later.	
	10.9.16		Bar 30.01 Ther 61 A quiet day. Observation conditions poor. Considerable firing Sentries of Crassier at intervals during the night. 2/Lt J.H FENNELL and A. SIMKINS are posted to 7th Division and leave to join	
	11.9.16		Bar 30. Ther 61. A quiet day except for a few 4.2's during the day. Also an out burst of 30 4.2's half of them Dud between 10.45 & 11.10 pm. Most of the shells dropped on railway between Quarry Bridge & Fosse 6.	
	12.9.16		Bar 29.96 Ther 59. Our T.M's are cutting wire S of Crassier in M10 c & M 9 d. Enemy made slight retaliation on our T.M's but we soon stopped his firing by retaliating on him. The enemy seems much more alert in his trenches no doubt by new troops and frightened at our wire cutting. 2/Lt A Morgan posted to 55th Div & leave to join.	
	13.9.16		Bar 29.9 Ther 60. A quiet day - our TM's continue wire cutting. The enemy seems to be holding their trenches very strongly and to be well on the alert.	MWP

WAR DIARY or INTELLIGENCE SUMMARY

Army Form C. 2118

Place	Date	Hour	Summary of Events and Information	Remarks and references to Appendices
	14.		Bar 29.3 Ther 63. Enemy slightly more active. Shelled position of B/188 with 4" guns no damage done. Hostile sentries much more alert.	
	15th		Barometer 29.93 Ther 54. Our TM's continue wire cutting operations opposite Puits 16. Enemy retaliated with heavy TM's and we retaliated on their batteries N & S of Crassier. Otherwise all quiet. Enemy's artillery fire nil.	
	16th		Bar 29.97 Ther 58. We cleared up the gaps made by TM's opposite Puits 16 with 200 rounds of Shrapnel. Enemy took advantage of our fire to shell in the area of B/188 with two batteries one 4 inch gun & one of 4.2 hows. no damage done. V shaped gaps have been cut in parapets of trenches South of the Crassier. Capt Buchan posted to 7th Divn & leaves to join. Capt Gray resumes Command of A 188 Bde RFA. We barrage enemy's trenches for an hour during infantry raid which was not successful.	
	17th		Bar 29.97 Ther 58°. Very bad light. 128 Bds fired by A 181 at gaps M.9.c 03.83 the gaps is not finished. Enemy fire very quiet.	MF

WAR DIARY
or
INTELLIGENCE SUMMARY
(Erase heading not required.)

Army Form C. 2118

Instructions regarding War Diaries and Intelligence Summaries are contained in F. S. Regs., Part II. and the Staff Manual respectively. Title Pages will be prepared in manuscript.

Place	Date	Hour	Summary of Events and Information	Remarks and references to Appendices
	18th Sept		Bar 30.18 Ther 53. Very bad light, pouring rain. Major Sinclair (A 161) attempted to continue wire cutting but it was impossible to begin till 6 o'clock owing to the light and after 34 rounds had been fired a mine went up near Seaforth Crater and all Batteries had to turn on to it in order to enable the Infantry to consolidate the Crater which was successfully accomplished. Owing to the wire not being cut the Infantry Raid proposed for tonight did not take place. 2nd Lt. T. R. Graham is posted from C. 158 Bde to A 170 Bde and 2nd Lt. T. M. K. Humfray is posted from A 17 Bde to A 158 Bde RFA	
	19th Sept		Bar 29.7 Ther 57. Very quiet except for two bursts of fire by the Enemy on Maroc to which we retaliated. Lt Col Wilson proceeds on leave. Temp. Lt Col (Major) D. H. Gill R.F.A. takes command of the group during his absence and Major C. E. Vickery D.S.O O/C 168 Bde takes command of 158 Brigade.	
	20th		Bar 29.26 Ther 49. Enemy T.M. fire on trenches North of Crassier greatly increased. It is probable that he organised a show as a counter to our TM fire which has been continuing with intent for the past week. We retaliated heavily with salvos of A x with little effect and Percival's Howrs were put to watch Hostile H.T. Mor. firing.	

WAR DIARY
or
INTELLIGENCE SUMMARY
(Erase heading not required.)

Army Form C. 2118

Place	Date	Hour	Summary of Events and Information	Remarks and references to Appendices
	21st Sep		Bar. 29.8. Ther 52. A quiet day. Our Trench mortars carried out a Bombardment. 10 shots were fired from our H.T.M. in Maroc and we masked its fire by bursts of Shrapnel in places likely to be used by enemy as O.P.s. The enemy did not retaliate to our fire. The 3rd Divn is moving out and the 40th Divn is extending to take over the front now held by Rt Group 47th Divn. The 40th Divn will be organised in 3 groups Left Centre & Right. Their groups remain Right group Major Vichy taking over command of group during Lt Col Watson absence Col Gill goes to command new Left Group 40th D.A.	
	22nd Sep		Bar 30. Ther 51. A very quiet day.	
	23rd Sep		Bar. 30. Ther 50. A quiet day.	
	24th Sep		Bar 30.14 Ther 48. Top of Ruts it fell down owing to H.T.M. fire. A quiet day. Capt Percival fired 30 rounds as experiment at 4 similar gaps in enemy's parapet below Fosse Avenue. H.G.R.A. inspected had him are Gas cylinders here. There has been much observation work done with studies will be ready, we had studies but his experiment in which showed in this shewed it has possibly arisen for detonation undergrounds space. 46 Hows cooperated in Barrage established for minor operation in Col Roberts own Group.	

WAR DIARY or INTELLIGENCE SUMMARY

Army Form C. 2118

(Erase heading not required.)

Place	Date	Hour	Summary of Events and Information	Remarks and references to Appendices
28th			Bar. 29.91. Ther. 51. A quiet day. Two raids made by our infantry. (1) 9.15 p.m. Opposite Puits 16. Artillery opened intense bombardment at -2 zero time followed by Barrage for 30 minutes. Infantry entered the enemy trenches successfully but were unfortunate in finding no enemy. 10.10 p.m. Gas alarm from Right Group of 37th Divn on our left. 37th Divn Artillery fired heavily for an hour. There was no gas. (2) 11.30 p.m. Raid North of Triangle M.5.d.20.40. No preliminary bombardment but Barrage maintained for one hour. Infantry again successfully entered the enemy's trenches but were met with considerable opposition finding the front line manned. The enemy were probably on priors & on the look out owing to the gas alarm which affected them as much as it did us.	
29th			Bar. 29. Ther. 55. A very beautiful day. Weather very calm & bright. Observation conditions good. Tactical situation quiet. Warning sent from 1st Army that there is considerably more hostile movement behind the lines than normal. The following extra are received from 18 Gen Comdg 114th Inf Bde, dealing with the attack by Right Group 38 Divn during last night (28/29th) inners [...]	J.W.K.

P.W.K.

WAR DIARY
or
INTELLIGENCE SUMMARY

Army Form C. 2118

Place	Date	Hour	Summary of Events and Information	Remarks and references to Appendices
26th Sep.			Copy O.C. Right Group Both Battalions speak very highly of the accuracy & effect of the Arty. work last night. The Bombardment on right flank was most accurate & well distributed and the Infantry got up within 30 yards of the hostile front line with absolute safety which gave entire confidence in the shooting of the Artillery. This confidence will be of great value for future raids. I personally should like to thank the Artillery for their excellent work last night. 26/9/16 sd/ C. Cuncliffe Owen Br.Gen. Comd'g 119th Bde.	
27th	Sep.		Barometer 29.94 Ther. 65. A very quiet day.	

WAR DIARY or INTELLIGENCE SUMMARY

Army Form C. 2118

Place	Date	Hour	Summary of Events and Information	Remarks and references to Appendices
	28th Sep		Barzag. Thurs 6. Again a very quiet day.	
	29th Sep		Barzag. Thurs 29. Weather fine, observation conditions bad, a very quiet day.	
	30th Sep		Barzag. Thurs 30. A quiet day, batteries done but registration till evening. 8th Welsh Regt carry out a raid on hostile trenches making an entry at M5d08.65. Artillery cooperated by an intense bombardment on the front line & the posting Guns followed by a Barrage maintained for 50 minutes. The Infantry got into the hostile trenches within 2 minutes of Bombardment leaving Bombay and a bomb and officers to whilst they found no Germans in the trenches but one the bms fired at their army and disappeared. They brought back a helmet which bears an important identification as it bore a regimental number and a stock to what a rifle after firing rifle grenades. This successful raid goes to prove the evidence that the best way of getting the Infantry into the trenches is by having an intense bombardment of the front line. MWH

40

Vol 5

CONFIDENTIAL.

War Diary of
188 Brigade R.F.A.

from 1st October 1916 to 31st October 1916

Volume I.

—

[signature]
LIEUT.-COL., R.F.A.,
COMMANDING 188TH BRIGADE, R.F.A.

WAR DIARY or INTELLIGENCE SUMMARY

Army Form C. 2118

(Erase heading not required.)

Instructions regarding War Diaries and Intelligence Summaries are contained in F. S. Regs., Part II. and the Staff Manual respectively. Title Pages will be prepared in manuscript.

Place	Date	Hour	Summary of Events and Information	Remarks and references to Appendices
Oct 1st			Bar 29.92 Ther 52. Bright sunny dull later, very quiet day. 19th RWF made a raid. Their position right pa[r]ty Steyaert Farm at M6 b M100 25 75 Centre pa[r]ty M10a 67 40 to M10a 85 30 Left party M4 c 97 60. The Right party the main raid 3 officers + 29 OR. Centre party 1 O + 16 OR. Left 1 NCO 6 OR. Artillery cooperated in bombardment on objective of right party. 5 minutes bombardment of objective of centre party and then barrage of 60 minutes ground also headed by Right party. The enemy answered full infantry day into Right party. Found the trenches full manned. Centre party only got in one trench & another. The right enter and one [illegible] [illegible] [illegible] as got in. The raid generally [illegible] [illegible] [illegible] but if you want to get the Infantry in the only way is an intense bombardment in front of [illegible].	
Oct 2nd			Bar 30.09 Ther 57. Weather very bad all quite Quiet.	
Oct 3rd			Bar 30 Ther 52. Very rainy day. Practically no Artillery fire from either side all day Quiet.	
Oct 4th			Bar 30.01 Ther 52. A very wet morning. In the afternoon at Wisseloch the Life Guard 2/4 Div carried out a daylight raid there was fairly heavy Artillery fire from the Guns on our left and the enemy replied with considerable machine gun fire. In the afternoon also the 12th Hrs fired at the enemy TM when he opened [illegible] trouble firing on [illegible] [illegible] from M4 d 90.02. Although the 12th seem to go right into the [illegible] where the	

WAR DIARY or INTELLIGENCE SUMMARY

Army Form C. 2118

(Erase heading not required.)

Place	Date	Hour	Summary of Events and Information	Remarks and references to Appendices
	4th Oct		smoke of the mortar came from it still continued to fire, it is probably at the foot of a long tunnel and will only be knocked out by firing a shell right down the tunnel in the direction of its line of fire. There was a heavy T.M. duel on the 37th Div front south of CALLONNE for about 1½ hours from 3 to 4.30 pm. The weather continues very bad and observation conditions are very poor. Tonight C/158 leaves the Centre group and goes into action somewhere in the South in the XI Corps area. C161 Bde RFA which has been attached to the LEFT GROUP also goes to the same area. This necessitates a reshuffling of the 4th D.A. Groups. D188 (Capt. Perceval) loses a How. from his position which goes away with C158 Bde & mans the Lone Tree in Loos which was previously manned by C188. and the two guns from Capt. Lloyd's B178 go back with him to the Left Group and are lost to the Right Group. Right group now consists of 18 pdrs A188 & B188 one section of C178 at Lone Tree and one gun of B178 at CALLONNE. 4.5 Hows 3 Hows at Capt Perceval's Battery position and one How in Loos.	
	6th Oct		Bar 29.72 Ther 58. A very quiet day practically no firing.	
	7th Oct		Bar 29.78 Ther 60. Brig Gen [illegible] away with "K" Bty [illegible] who has been commanding the Bde. during the General's absence returns to the Right Group and takes over command from Major [illegible] D.S.O.	

WAR DIARY or INTELLIGENCE SUMMARY

Army Form C. 2118

(Erase heading not required.)

Instructions regarding War Diaries and Intelligence Summaries are contained in F. S. Regs., Part II. and the Staff Manual respectively. Title Pages will be prepared in manuscript.

Place	Date	Hour	Summary of Events and Information	Remarks and references to Appendices
	6th Oct (cont)		[illegible]	
	7 Oct		Bar 29.09 Therm 62. All quiet [illegible]	
	8 Oct		[illegible handwritten entries regarding bombardment, WINGLES, positions]	
	9 Oct		Bar [illegible] Therm 60. All quiet [illegible] Lt. R. H. Webb D/188 evacuated sick [illegible]	
	10 Oct		Bar 30.09 Therm 58. [illegible] Section [illegible] B/188 [illegible] at M.14.d.00.85 and put into two guns into position at G.26.c.70.30	

WAR DIARY or INTELLIGENCE SUMMARY

Army Form C. 2118

Instructions regarding War Diaries and Intelligence Summaries are contained in F. S. Regs., Part II. and the Staff Manual respectively. Title Pages will be prepared in manuscript.

(Erase heading not required.)

Place	Date	Hour	Summary of Events and Information	Remarks and references to Appendices
	11th Oct		Bar 30.08 Ther 58. A very quiet day. The 40th Division front is to be extended to the North up to and including Boyan 77. The Right group takes over the LOOS SECTION covering a front from double Crassier to LOOS CRASSIER. The Right group is reconstituted and gets another Battery A 181 it will contain A188 • Removes completely to G.26.c.20.30 B188 } Remain in their present positions D188 } A181 Remains in its position at G.33.a.4.0.75 Relief complete at 7.30 p.m. 11th/12th.	
	12 Oct		Bar 30.08 Ther 59. Relief completed. Right Group taken over the LOOS SECTION. The 119th Infantry Bde. still in front of us. All very quiet, slightly more mortar activity.	
	13th Oct		Bar 30.14 Thermom 61. A quiet day.	
	14th Oct		Bar 30.9 Thermom 58. Enemy trench mortars active during the afternoon chiefly from South of Crassier we were obliged with the leave of left group 37th Divn to fire into their area.	
	15th Oct		Bar 30.12 Thermom 69. Enemy trench mortars still rather active in the morning otherwise a quiet uneventful day.	

WAR DIARY or INTELLIGENCE SUMMARY

Army Form C. 2118

(Erase heading not required.)

Place	Date	Hour	Summary of Events and Information	Remarks and references to Appendices
	16th Oct		Bar 29.74 Thermom 55. A quiet day.	
	17th Oct		Bar 30.08 Thermom 47. The enemy very heavily bombarded our trenches with Trench Mortar fire all along the Loos Section front. A great deal of fire was directed over the Crassier by mortars situated on the South & though these were heavily engaged by the 37th Division Arty still continued to fire. Our retaliation both on the front line and on suspected mortar emplacements had little effect & the enemy continued to fire until a Howitzer Battery was put on to demolish a selected piece of Trench. The day otherwise was quiet	
	18th Oct		Bar 30.09. Thermom 45. A quiet day and night. The division on our right (the 37th) is relieved by the 2nd Canadian Division.	
	19th Oct		Bar 29.76 Thermom 54. C Battery returned from XIth Corps rejoins the Div'n and comes into the Right Group at its old position at G.32.d.30.00. With 3 Hows. One How goes to Capt Perceval in his position and Major Hill takes over two Hows in the CHALK PIT.	Map

WAR DIARY or INTELLIGENCE SUMMARY

Army Form C. 2118

(Erase heading not required.)

Instructions regarding War Diaries and Intelligence Summaries are contained in F. S. Regs., Part II. and the Staff Manual respectively. Title Pages will be prepared in manuscript.

Place	Date	Hour	Summary of Events and Information	Remarks and references to Appendices
	20th Oct		Baro 29.79 Thermo 50. Quiet day minor operation between 19th R.W.F. 8.30 - 9.30. Barrage. Infantry enter trenches and obtain identifications.	
	21st Oct		Baro 30.14 Thermo 37. A very quiet day - few aeroplane targets ranged. Very good shooting by Capt Perceval. A 181 shelled with 5.9's from direction of LENS and at 9.33 a 40 75-- from true bearing 137½°°	
	22nd Oct		Baro 29.9 Thermo 35. Heavy frost during the night a quiet day except for a little TM firing near HARRISSONS CRATER. on which we retaliated heavily.	
	23rd Oct		Baro 29.68 Thermo 43. A very quiet day. Mostly unusual in front.	
	24th Oct		Baro 29.91 Thermo 43. A quiet day Hun slightly more active with TM's	
	25th Oct		Baro 29.69 Thermo 48 The Hun quiet Infantry ask for retaliation for TM's though the Enemy have not been very active. We retaliate in conjunction with heavies.	
	26th		Baro 29.36 Thermo 49. Very bad weather a quiet day.	

MK.

WAR DIARY or INTELLIGENCE SUMMARY

Army Form C. 2118

Instructions regarding War Diaries and Intelligence Summaries are contained in F. S. Regs., Part II. and the Staff Manual respectively. Title Pages will be prepared in manuscript.

(Erase heading not required.)

Place	Date	Hour	Summary of Events and Information	Remarks and references to Appendices
	27th Oct		Baro 29.58 Thermo 49. The enemy showed increased T.M. activity and was heavily strafed by us. Otherwise a quiet rainy day. Lt. M. McGillewie is transferred to the R.G.A. & is posted to 184 Siege Battery. The four following officers join the Brigade and are posted to the Batteries against their names. 2nd Lt. F.W. Cooper to A 188. Temp Lieut H.L. WEBBER to B 188. Temp 2nd Lieut W. SCOTT MONCRIEFF (SR) to C 188. Lieut H. MITTON to D 188.	
	28th Oct		Baro 29.54 Thermo 47. A very quiet 24 hours all activity below normal.	
	29th Oct		Baro 29.47 Thermo 52. All quiet quiet the 119th Brigade are relieved by 73rd Bde of 24th Div.	
	30th Oct		Baro 29.46 Thermo 45. Enemy slightly more active with T.M's heavily retaliated on by us and silenced.	
	31st Oct		Baro 29.65 Thermo 48 A very quiet day. 2nd Lieut C.D. Rutherford rejoins the Brigade and goes to B 188.	MR

WAR DIARY
or
INTELLIGENCE SUMMARY
(Erase heading not required.)

Army Form C. 2118

188th Bde RFA Vol 6

Place	Date	Hour	Summary of Events and Information	Remarks and references to Appendices
	1st Nov. 1916		Barom 29.65 Thermom 48 - Everything exceptionally quiet on our front.	
	2nd		Baro 29.92 Thermom 48. A quiet day. Lt W.J. Price of D188 posted to B 178 Bde. 2nd Lt R.F.T. Allen of B178 posted to B178 Bde.	
	3rd		Baro 29.92 Thermo 52. Another quiet day. 2Lt S.T. Ralph-Smith posted from B 188 Bde to C 178 Bde. 2Lt W.K. Horsfall posted from C 178 Bde to B 178 Bde.	
	4th		Barom. 29.71 Thermom 47. Quiet all along our front.	
	5th		Barom 29.44 Thermom 52. All quiet. Major William Frederick Parsons arrives and takes over command of the Brigade and Right Group	WFP

WAR DIARY
or
INTELLIGENCE SUMMARY
(Erase heading not required.)

Army Form C. 2118

Place	Date	Hour	Summary of Events and Information	Remarks and references to Appendices
	6. Nov 16		Barometer 29.07 Thermom 54. Quiet day. Lt A Stonehouse is substituted for Lt St Ralph Smith. and	
	7th Nov.		Barometer 29.45 Therm. m 49. Our H.T.M in Loos shot on the enemy's trenches south east of Loos Crassier. A181 6guns & C.188 cooperated shortly on trenches & trench junctions in the vicinity in order to cover the TM fire. Stokes guns and medium TM's joined in the bombardment. The H.T.M started fire at 2.30 and fired off its rounds at set intervals previously arranged the artillery bombarding for two minutes starting a minute before each round went off. The shoot was very effective only marred by the H.T.M dropping one round short in our support line. The Enemy made slight Mortar Retaliation.	
	8 Nov.		Barom 29.3 Thermom 46. A Quiet day. The Canadian Arty on our right assisted by the Heavies Bombarded the Mortar emplacements & trenches to the South of the Double Crassier	
				MLP

WAR DIARY or INTELLIGENCE SUMMARY

Army Form C. 2118

(Erase heading not required.)

Place	Date	Hour	Summary of Events and Information	Remarks and references to Appendices
	9th Nov		Baro 29.7 Thermo 45. A quiet 24 hours. Field Marshall H.R.H the Duke of Connaught K.G. etc. inspected the gun position of Major C.E.Mckay oc B188. The field marshall was accompanied by 7 other generals, including the Army Commander, Corps Commander, Army & Corps R.A. Commander the BGRA. The Duke expressed himself as highly pleased with all he saw. He went over all the Batty position into the Gun pits & Officers mess. At midnight the position of Adjutant was relinquished by Temp Lt N.W. Freeman on posting to A Battery 188 Bde. He had held the position of adjutant in the Brigade since 26th Feby 1916. Temp Lt Mann the Orderly Officer takes on the duties of adjutant from 0.00. am 10th Nov. NWF.	

WAR DIARY or INTELLIGENCE SUMMARY

Army Form C. 2118

Place	Date	Hour	Summary of Events and Information	Remarks and references to Appendices
	10th Nov 1916		Baro- 30.1 Thermom. 49. A very quiet day – Three of our Batteries A. C. and D/188 carried out some aeroplane ranging –	
	11th		Baro- 30.19 Thermom 49. Another quiet day. Major C Vickery D.S.O. R.F.A warned to proceed tomorrow 12th to attend Conference at BOULOGNE for about one week.	
	12th		Baro- 30.24 Thermom. 52. Conference of B.Cs at Group H.Q. Discussion on recent Artillery orders issued on SOMME, particularly with regard to creeping barrages. Some difficulty being experienced by T.M. Batteries in finding labour – owing to the Infantry being so busy in repair of their trenches consequent on the bad weather. The Right Group is now providing 12 men per 18 Pr Bty & 8 men per How Bty as a bomb-carrying fatigue – The Group on our Right carried out this afternoon a scheme for knocking out M. Gun & T.M. emplacements.	

WAR DIARY or INTELLIGENCE SUMMARY

Army Form C. 2118

(Erase heading not required.)

Place	Date	Hour	Summary of Events and Information	Remarks and references to Appendices
	Nov 13th	10.a.m	Barom. 30.2 Thermom. 52°. The Group Commander attended conference held at Centre Groups H.Q. presided over by G.O.C.R.A. 40th Div. A quiet day all along our front. Observation conditions poor nearly all day.	
	Nov 14	8.45.a.m	Barom. 30.24 Thermom. 51°. ARTILLERY ROW was shelled with 21 - 4.2s, most of them however fell short. No damage done to O.Ps. Name of Major G. N. HILL. R.G.A submitted for Staff appointment to G.O.C. of a Corps. Name of Capt W.S. WINGATE GRAY submitted for Brigade Major to Div. Art. Name of MAJOR C. VICKERY D.S.O. R.F.A again forwarded for G.S.O.2.	
	15th		Barom 30.27 Thermom. 37°. A fairly quiet day. Battery Commanders attended a very interesting lecture at CENTRE GROUP H.Q. by BDE MAJ. 21st DIV. R.A. (CAPT PAGE R.F.A) on recent experiences of the fighting and conditions on the SOMME	

WAR DIARY or INTELLIGENCE SUMMARY

Army Form C. 2118

Place	Date	Hour	Summary of Events and Information	Remarks and references to Appendices
	Nov 16.		Barom 30.26 Thermom 36°
A very quiet day - Observation conditions poor.	
	17		Barom 29.79 Thermom 29°
Another quiet day. An aeroplane from our affiliated squadron ranged for 2 of the Batteries. One Section of 18 pdrs from A/188 joined Buxton Group.	
	18		Barom. 28.74 Thermom 30°
Lt WEBBER transferred from B/188 to 40th D.A.C.
We fired on new work carried out by enemy as well as his periscopes & O.P.
For some time past, hostile artillery fire has been almost negligible on our Sector.
Test rockets were sent up last night & were successfully treated.	
	19		Barom. 28.64 Thermom 40°
1st Corps Heavies carried out a bombardment of enemy front line between DOUBLE CRASSIER and LOOS CRASSIER.
ARTILLERY ROW was shelled with about 30 rounds from 4" gun. Several direct hits.	

WAR DIARY
or
INTELLIGENCE SUMMARY

Army Form C. 2118

Instructions regarding War Diaries and Intelligence Summaries are contained in F. S. Regs., Part II. and the Staff Manual respectively. Title Pages will be prepared in manuscript.

(Erase heading not required.)

Place	Date	Hour	Summary of Events and Information	Remarks and references to Appendices
Nov.	20.		Barom 29.27 Thermom. 39°. Enemy rather more active with Trench Mortars and 7.75. Our two 4.5 How. Batteries fired on and destroyed portions of enemy trenches.	
	21.		Barom 29.37 Thermom 38. LT FREEMAN & LT HORSFALL proceed to ENGLAND on course of instruction. A very quiet day. Observation conditions poor on account of mist.	
	22		Barom 29.68. Thermom 40. An unusually quiet day.	
	23.		Barom 29.65 Thermom 43°. MAJOR HILL proceeds on leave. Nothing of importance to note.	
	24.		Barom 30.09 Thermom 44°. Revised schemes prepared for dealing with gas attack.	

WAR DIARY or INTELLIGENCE SUMMARY

Army Form C. 2118

(Erase heading not required.)

Place	Date	Hour	Summary of Events and Information	Remarks and references to Appendices
Nov.	24	Cont'd	MAJOR SINCLAIR proceeds to BETHUNE to report to 6th Div. & takes over temporary duties of Bde Major to Composite Artillery Div. LIEUT WHITTLE is put in temporary command of A.181. MAJOR C.E. VICKERY proceeds to ENGLAND to report to War Office. LIEUT. S. RALPH-SMITH is put in temporary command of B/188.	
	25		Barom 29.81. Thermom. 50 Our Hows shelled selected T.M. emplacements in retaliation for enemy T.M. activity. Otherwise a quiet day.	
	26		Barom. 29.51 Thermom 40 Three men of B/188 wounded slightly — near FOSSE 7. D.188 again shelled T.M. emplacement which had been active near HARRISONS CRATER.	

WAR DIARY or INTELLIGENCE SUMMARY

Army Form C. 2118

(Erase heading not required.)

Place	Date	Hour	Summary of Events and Information	Remarks and references to Appendices
	Nov. 27th		Barom. 29.81 Thermom. 38. Trench boards marked E. H. and L. have now been fixed in front line trenches and are visible from O.Ps. A few 5.9s fell round FOSSE 7 and caused some casualties in the adjoining Group. LT MITTON R.F.A. posted to 24th D.A. O.C Group reconnoitred for & reported on position for a new Tower O.P (Position M.3.b.60.55)	
	28th		Barom 30.29 Thermom. 34. LT H.T.P. MOORE granted leave as well as 5 O.R. Aeroplanes on both sides were most active, observation conditions were extremely good. Bombs were dropped near FOSSE 7 by enemy aeroplanes, causing ce casualties in adjoining Groups. Sergt JOLLY C. of D/188 has been awarded the Military Medal. 2/LIEUT. T. E. EVESON R.F.A from 24th D.A.C. posted to D/188. COL WALTHALL commanding Rt Group 24th D.A. who will be relieving us, was shown round all Battery positions & Group H.Q.	
	29th		Barom 30.33 Thermom 32. A very quiet day. Our Infantry fired a Bangalore Torpedo in enemy wire near point of Triangle — One	

WAR DIARY or INTELLIGENCE SUMMARY

Army Form C. 2118

Place	Date	Hour	Summary of Events and Information	Remarks and references to Appendices
Nov.	29th	Cont'd	of our Batteries fired salvoes into enemy trenches in rear and evidently caused him a certain amount of anxiety, judging by his reply with aerial darts & T.Ms.	
	30th		Barom. 30.09 Thermom. 32°. The enemy early this morning was very active in vicinity of Triangle with T.Ms. Observation conditions have been unfavourable for the past few days, owing to fogs and ground mists. A Revised scheme for support of CENTRE GROUP, having been approved by 40th D.A. was sent out to Batteries concerned. Hostile Artillery throughout this month has been insignificant.	

L.T. Parsons
Major
188th Bde R.F.A.

WAR DIARY or INTELLIGENCE SUMMARY

148 BDE. R.F.A.

Vol 7

Place	Date	Hour	Summary of Events and Information	Remarks and references to Appendices
	1916 Dec 1		Barom. 30·02 Thermom. 33 Orders issued to Batteries in connection with coming move. O.C. attended a conference at CENTRE GROUP H.Q. presided over by B.G.R.A. 40th. "DUNDEE" was fired at 4.20 p.m.	
	2		Barom. 29·90 Thermom. 35 A quiet day – Hostile T.Ms were active in afternoon by HARRISONS CRATER, we retaliated with 4·5 Hows. MAJOR SINCLAIR returned from 6th DIV & took over his Bty.	
	3		Barom. 29·85 Thermom. 33 Another quiet day – Practically no Artillery fire – The Orderly Officer of the 108 Bde. R.F.A. arrived to take over telephone lines from us, bringing 3 signallers with him to take over the exchange. Sections of the relieving batteries arrived and our sections pulled out; this relief was completed by 7·0 p.m. Our Orderly Officer proceeding to MARLES-LES-MINES this morning with billetting party.	

WAR DIARY or INTELLIGENCE SUMMARY

Army Form C. 2118

(Erase heading not required.)

Place	Date	Hour	Summary of Events and Information	Remarks and references to Appendices
	Dec 3	Cont.d	Our Sections (4 Guns per 6 gun 18 P.R Bty & 2 Hows per Bty) marched over this evening to MARLES-LES-MINES. F.B. and first line wagons, together with Supply wagons left wagon lines for same destination at 2 p.m. All ammunition is being left behind. Wagons go light. The 2 15-Pdrs in LOOS were handed over by an Officer of C/184 this afternoon to Ord. Off of 108th Bde.	
	Dec 4		COL. WALTHALL R.F.A. with his Adjutant & H.Q. Staff arrived this morning to relieve us. All schemes, maps and fixtures were handed over. The remaining sections of Batteries were relieved this evening. All reliefs completed by 6.p.m. Batteries & H.Q. marched independently for our first destination by following route. NOEUX-LES-MINES - HAILLICOURT - MARLES LES MINES. Good billets were found for men & shelter for horses. Only 1 casualty on the road. (a horse with a picked up nail.	
	5		Orders issued to Batteries for march tomorrow. Orderly Officer with billeting party went off to MONCHY BRETON. All Batteries filled up with ammunition. Major G.N HILL is in temporary command of the Brigade owing to indisposition of MAJOR PARSONS.	
	6		The Brigade moved off at 8.40 a.m in the following order Bde H.Q. Staff A.C.B.D. by following route CALONNE RICOUART - CAMBLAIN CHÂTELAIN - DIVION - OURION - DIÉVAL - BRYAS - OSTREVILLE - MARQUAY. where the Bde is billetted for the night. Time of arrival 2.15. p.m.	

WAR DIARY or INTELLIGENCE SUMMARY

(Erase heading not required.)

Army Form C. 2118

Place	Date	Hour	Summary of Events and Information	Remarks and references to Appendices
	Dec 7		The Brigade moved off from MARQUAY billeting area at 9-20.a.m. in following order H.Q. Staff C.B.-A.D.B.15. Route followed OSTREVILLE - ST. POL - HERLIN le Sec. - ECOIVRES - FLERS - MONCHEL CONCHY sur Canche - Distance covered about 15 miles - Arrived at billeting area at 3-15.p.m. 10 minute halt were made every hour - The last 6 miles of the journey was heavy going for the horses. Major G.N.HILL is still in temporary command of the Bde.	
	8.		The Brigade left billeting area of MONCHEL at 8.50.a.m. & marched to AUTHIEULE by following route - BOUBERS.sur.Canche - LIGNY.sur.Canche - FREVENT - BOUQUEMAISON. DOULLENS. Order of march as follows. Bde. Staff B.D.A.C. The horse lines here are a perfect quagmire - We arrived at billets at 3.10.p.m. - Horses were watered and fed at BOUQUEMAISON.	
	9		The Bde. left billeting area at 11.15.a.m. & marched to TALMAS via DOULLENS & BEAUVAL arriving there about 4.p.m. MAJOR PARSONS rejoined us on the march & again took command. Our Interpreter ordered to report to Col ALLEN 178 Bde.	
	10		The Bde. left TALMAS at 8.50 and marched to AIRAINES via NAOURS. WARGNIES. HAVERNAS VIGNACOURT. BOURDON. HANGEST. & arrived in billeting area at 4.15.p.m. Reported on arrival to 40th D.A. also to 8th Div. The horses stood the march uncommonly well. They are being picquetted in the open on account of recent cases of mange among the French horses. This town is being used as a collecting station for sick horses of the French army. The men are all in billets.	

WAR DIARY or INTELLIGENCE SUMMARY

Army Form C. 2118

(Erase heading not required.)

Instructions regarding War Diaries and Intelligence Summaries are contained in F. S. Regs., Part II. and the Staff Manual respectively. Title Pages will be prepared in manuscript.

Place	Date	Hour	Summary of Events and Information	Remarks and references to Appendices
	Dec 11		A very large Sick parade this morning, the weather throughout the march has been wet & bad colds and rheumatism are the result. Batteries are improving billets, horse standings etc. A picket provided for patrolling the town. Arrangements made for baths.	
	12		Authority obtained from 8th Div. for drawing on D.A.D.O.S. & R.Es of their Division. Supplies are being drawn from L'ARBRE LA MOUCHES. Visit from BRIG GENl NICHOLSON comdg R.A. 8th Div. Programme for training being drawn up. Arranged for instructor of signallers & T.M. Batteries. T.Ms also supplying own Batteries with fatigue parties.	
	13.		Field Genl Court Martial at ALLERY presided over by Col DUNLOP R.F.A for trial of 2 men of D/188. for drunkenness. B.G.R.A. 40th Div. visited the Brigade.	
	14		All Batteries busy in improving Stabling and billets. Arrangements made for purchase of straw for mens billets. Drying rooms prepared for men & an extra supply of fuel obtained for same.	
	15		Visit from Gen NICHOLSON. Programmes for training for forthcoming week prepared & sent in to 8th Div. Plan received from 8th Div showing training area. Copies sent to each Bty.	
	16-17		Physical Drill and general fatigues. Reconnoitring for Rifle and revolver ranges, drill grounds etc.	
	18		Church Parade. Site selected for stable building. Trees bought for this purpose & wagons loaned from D.A.C.	
	19		Commencement made with stabling. Training commences today. A further 500 trees bought for stabling. Our D.H. has moved to HALLENCOURT.	
	20-2oth		Daily programme of physical drill. Gun Drill. Lectures. driving drill & football. All Batteries busy in turn felling and carting timber also carting chalk for stabling and erecting stabling for 2 Batteries. Arrangements made for all units for Div. Baths weekly.	
	24		Combined 188 Bde & 40th T.M. Concert at HOTEL DE FRANCE.	
	25.		Church parade in MARKET SQ. AIRAINES for 166 & 188 Bdes. also T.Ms. All Batteries & H.Q. were given a good Xmas dinner.	

WAR DIARY or INTELLIGENCE SUMMARY

Army Form C. 2118

Instructions regarding War Diaries and Intelligence Summaries are contained in F. S. Regs., Part II. and the Staff Manual respectively. Title Pages will be prepared in manuscript.

(Erase heading not required.)

Place	Date	Hour	Summary of Events and Information	Remarks and references to Appendices
	Dec. 26.		Holiday — Football matches. 1. Officers 9/188 v. Officers 40th T.M. 2. Men 9/188 v. Men of 40th T.M.	
	27th		All arrangements made for forward march. Units from 4th 8th 33rd & 40th Divs are moving up towards COMBLES and are proceeding by ½ Batteries of all units except D/188 which moves complete with 1st half groups. Orders by LIEUT. COL. PARSONS issued to all units concerned. COL. PARSONS will be in command of Column on 1st day — MAJOR G.N.HILL the 2nd day.	
	28.		The column moved off from AIRAINES at 9. a.m. starting point X Roads at LEQUESNOY — order of march. H.Q. 188. H.Q. 166. A.B.D. 166. A.D.B.C 188. 66. 88. 86 Bde. 4th Div. D.Z. D5. R.H.A. 8th Div. Route SOUES. PICQUIGNY. BREILLY. AILLY. ST.SAUVEUR. arrived at 2.30 p.m. Distance about 14 miles. H.Q. established at the School ST SAUVEUR. — Good billetting.	
	29.		The Column moved off at 8. a.m. order of march. H.Q. D.C.B.A. 188 — D5. Z.O. B½ 5th R.H.A Bd. 88. 86. 68 Bde 14th Bde. R.F.A. H.Q. D.B.A. 166 — H.Q. 8th Div Train S.R.E.s. Transport 8th Div. Route LONGPRÉ. AMIENS. VECQUEMONT. FOUILLOY. CORBIE. VAUX. arrived at 3.25 p.m. Billetting area very crowded —	
	30		The Column moved off for CAMP. 14 (BOIS de Taille) at 9 a.m — starting point fork roads 100x W of S in SAILLY le Sec thence on to main CORBIE-BRAY Road to CAMP. 14 — arriving at 12.30 —	
	31		The Bde. marched independently to Wagon lines ½ mile N.E. of SUZANNE near BRAY arriving at 11.30 a.m. and ½ Bties took over from 178 Bde. — The Colonel moved on to H.Q. with him, the detachment of ½ Batteries will proceed by Motor bus tomorrow —	
	1917 Jan. 1.		Took over from 178 Bde. R.F.A. and reported all reliefs complete to 40th D.A. — Our part of the line is E of RANCOURT — we cover the Right Batt. Left Bde Rt. Div. and are responsible for enemy front line S.W. of ST PIERRE VAAST WOOD from C.3.d.35.40 — C.2.b.99.35. We only have 3 of our Batteries in the line A B and C/188 — D/188 remaining behind at CAMP. 14. A/188 relieved C/178 at FREGICOURT B/188 relieved B/178. and C/188 relieved D/178. close to ARDERLU WOOD. H.Q. established S.E. Corner of the wood —	H. Parsons Lt Col Comdg 188 Bde R.F.A. W.J. Parsons Lt Col Comdg 188th Bde R.F.A

1875 Wt. W593/826 1,000,000 4/15 J.B.C. & A. A.D.S.S./Forms/C. 2118.

www.ingramcontent.com/pod-product-compliance
Lightning Source LLC
Chambersburg PA
CBHW081239170426
43191CB00034B/1983